the Andy Griffith Show

Bewitched

SPELLS

The Beverly
HILLBILLIES

BARNEY MILLER

BATMAN

THE
DICK VAN DYKE
SHOW

F TROOP

ALL
IN THE
FAMILY

THE Ed SULLIVAN
SHOW

THE
BEATLES

GILLIGAN'S
ISLAND

BONANZA

The
LOVE
BOAT

The
Carol Burnett
Show

I Love Lucy

your

HOGAN'S HEROES

HAZEL

I DREAM of JEANNIE

Timmy &
Lassie

GUNSMOKE

LOST
IN
SPACE

M*A*S*H

LOS ANGELES
BURBANK 5610 MILES
DECATUR
FRANCISCO
NAPOLIS 6779 MILES

THE MUNSTERS

That Girl

STAR TREK

THE FLYING NUN

THE
Lone Ranger

THE ADVENTURES OF
SUPERMAN

The Addams Family

63915951R00024

Made in the USA
Middletown, DE
06 February 2018